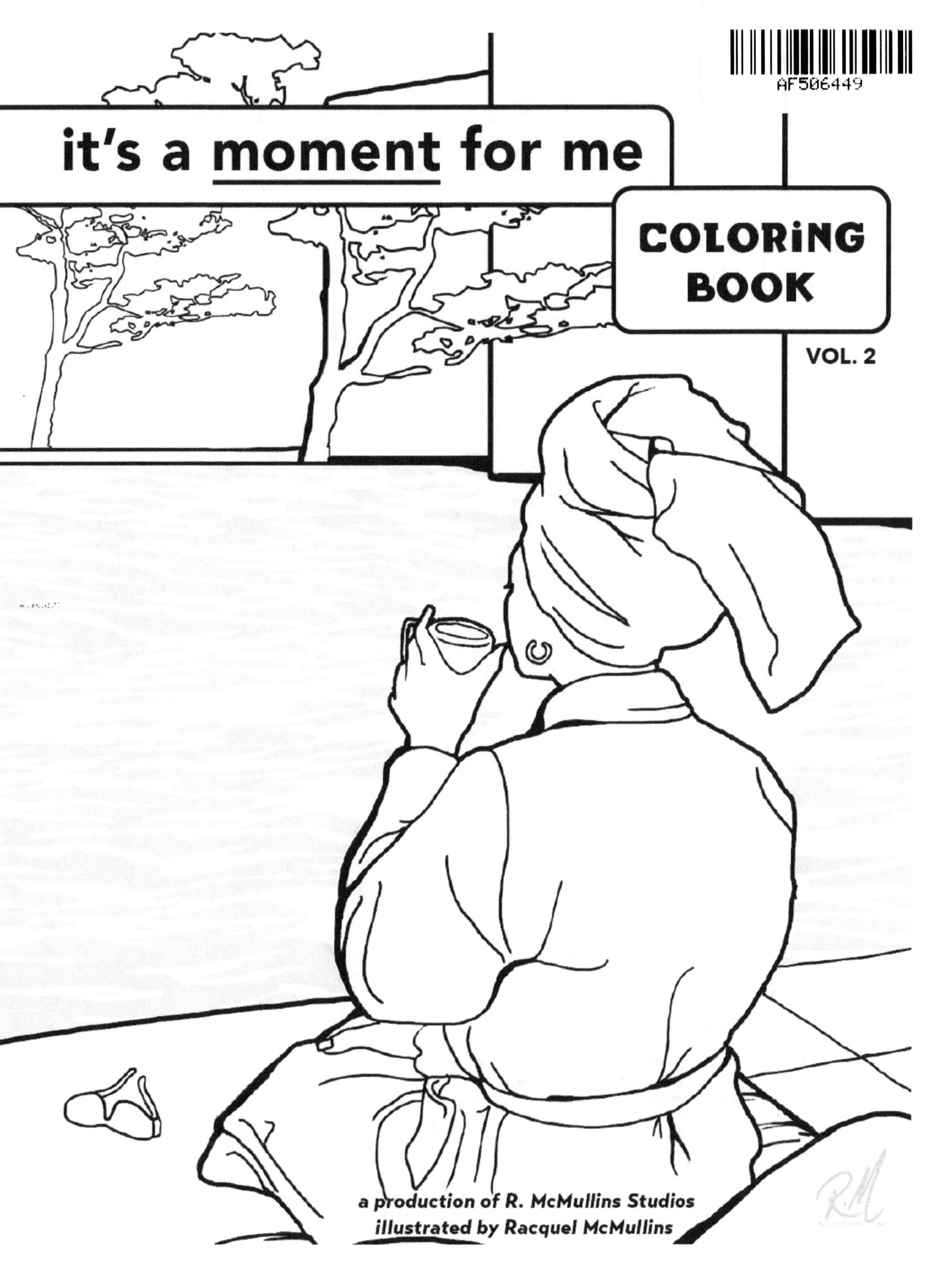
AF506449
it's a moment for me
COLORiNG BOOK
VOL. 2
a production of R. McMullins Studios
illustrated by Racquel McMullins

Designs by R. McMullins Studios LLC © 2022

Here we are for round two of "it's a moment for me".
Welcome back!!! I'm excited you came back. And for
those who are here for the first time, enjoy the moment.

These illustrations show the peace, love, and joy that
comes when we take a moment for ourselves. Use these
coloring pages as an opportunity to take a moment for
yourself. You deserve a moment of stillness.

As you color the pages be intentional about the time you
are spending. Bring the illustrations to life. Manifest the
self-love needed to thrive! Seek the peace found within!
Bask in the courage and kindness it takes to make time
for **YOU!**

The kids want to color with you too!

We've heard several stories where the kids took over your moment. They wanted to color right along with you. Hence, they took over your pages. To help with that we created a kid's edition. Below you will see certain page numbers that match up with the kid's edition.

it's a moment for me (**ADULT**)   it's a moment for me (**KIDS**)

	(A)	(K)
Dance with Me	51	5
Skate Time	53	9
Puppy	33	13
Purse	17	19
Dragonfly	65	25

matching pages are   #

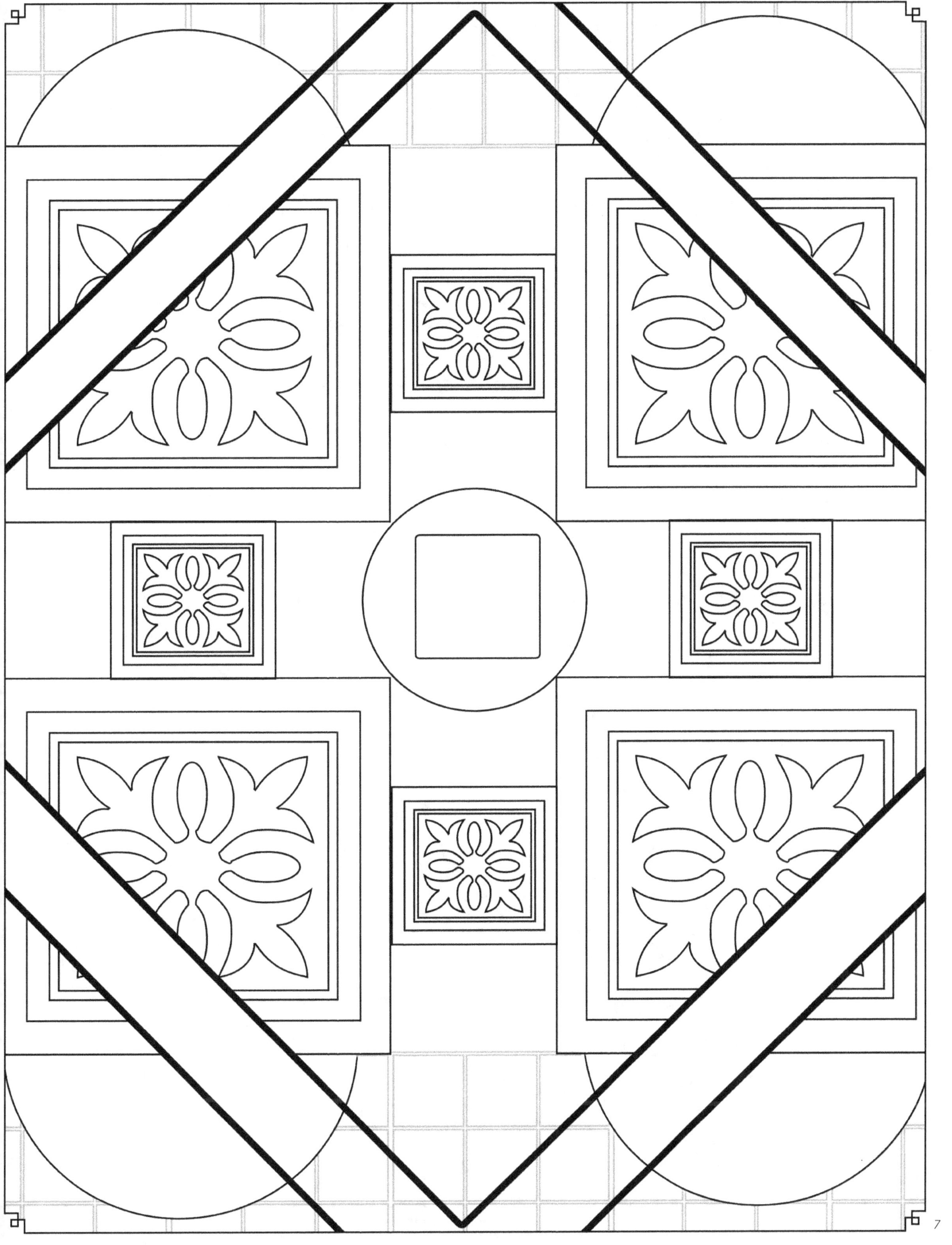

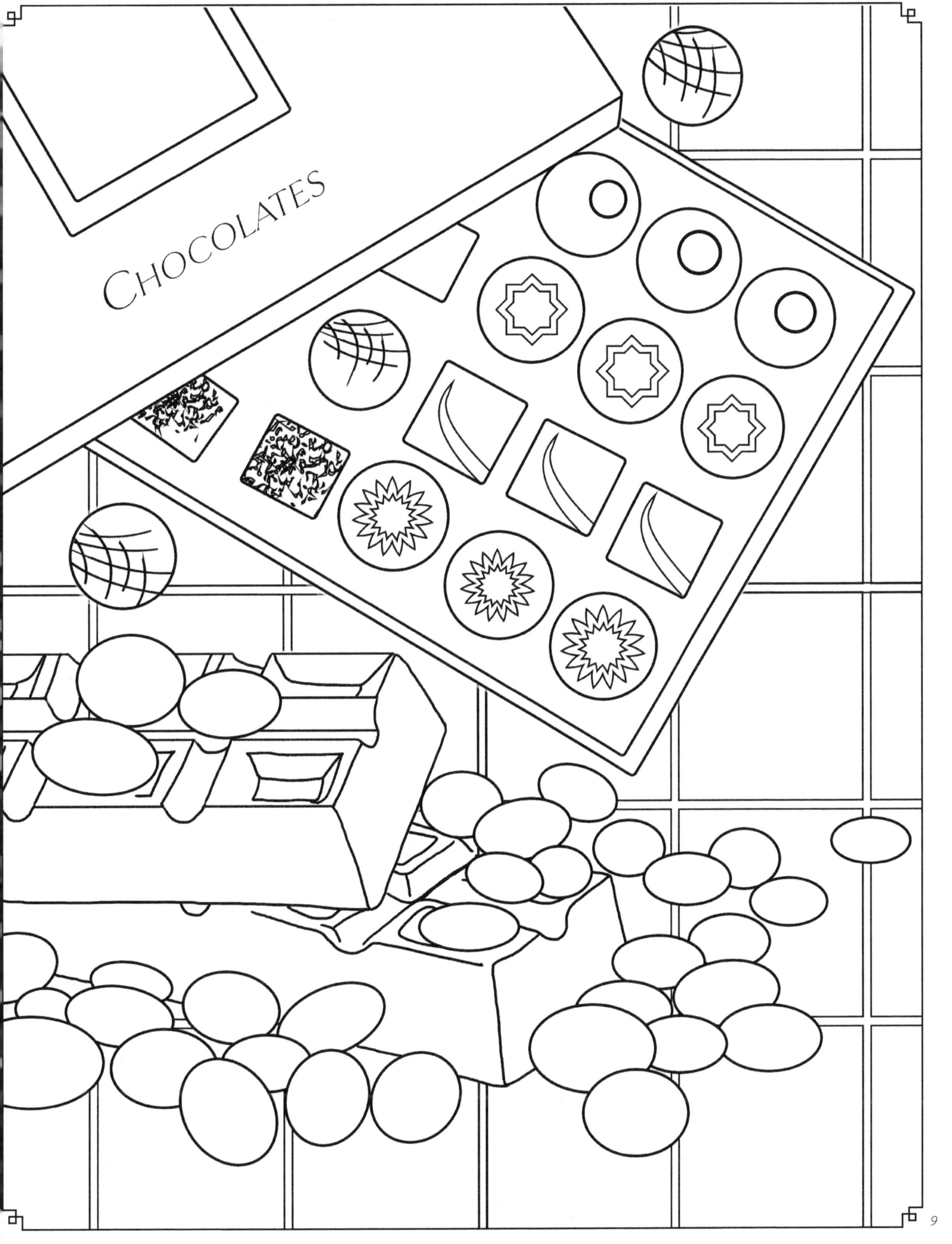

CHOCOLATES

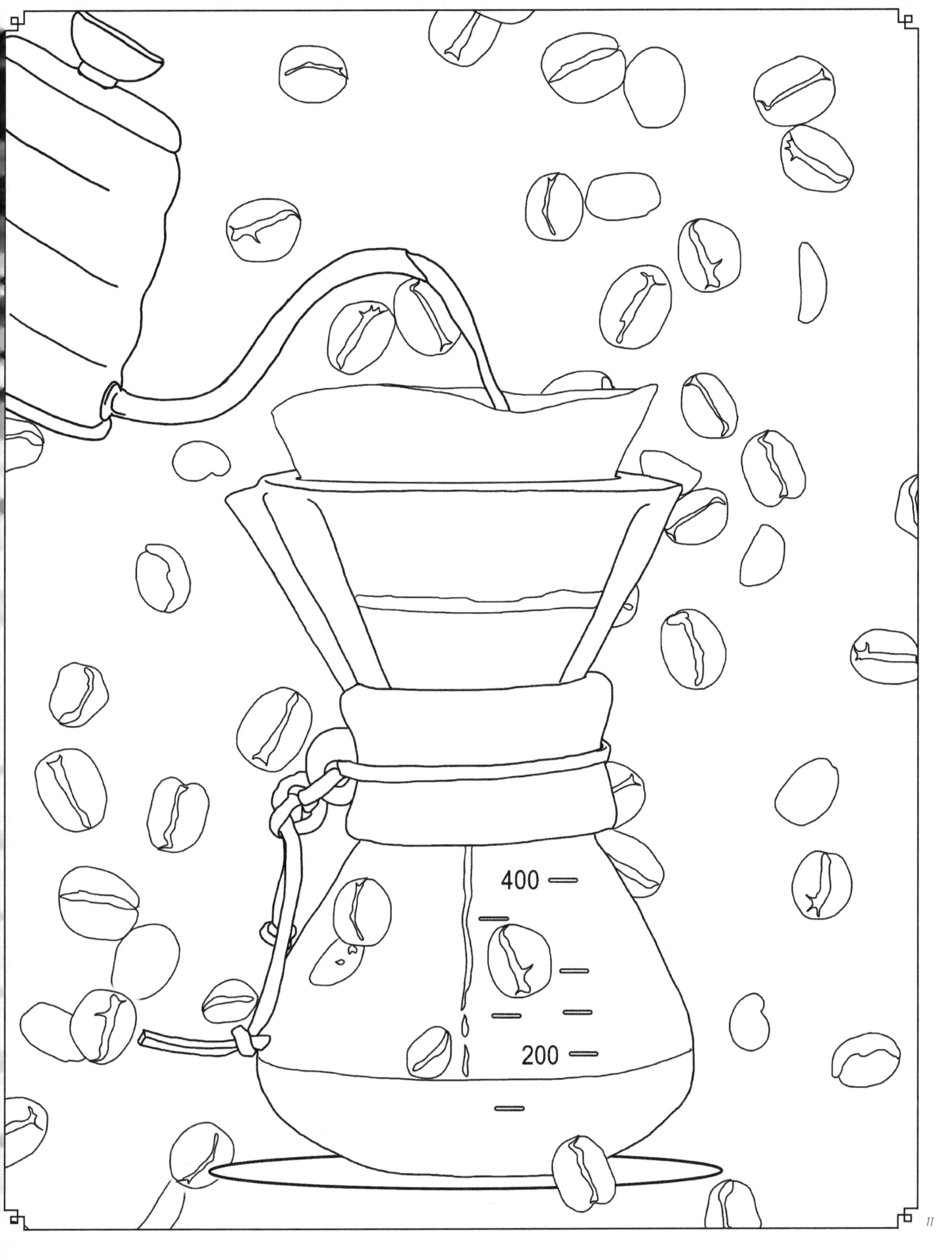

400
200

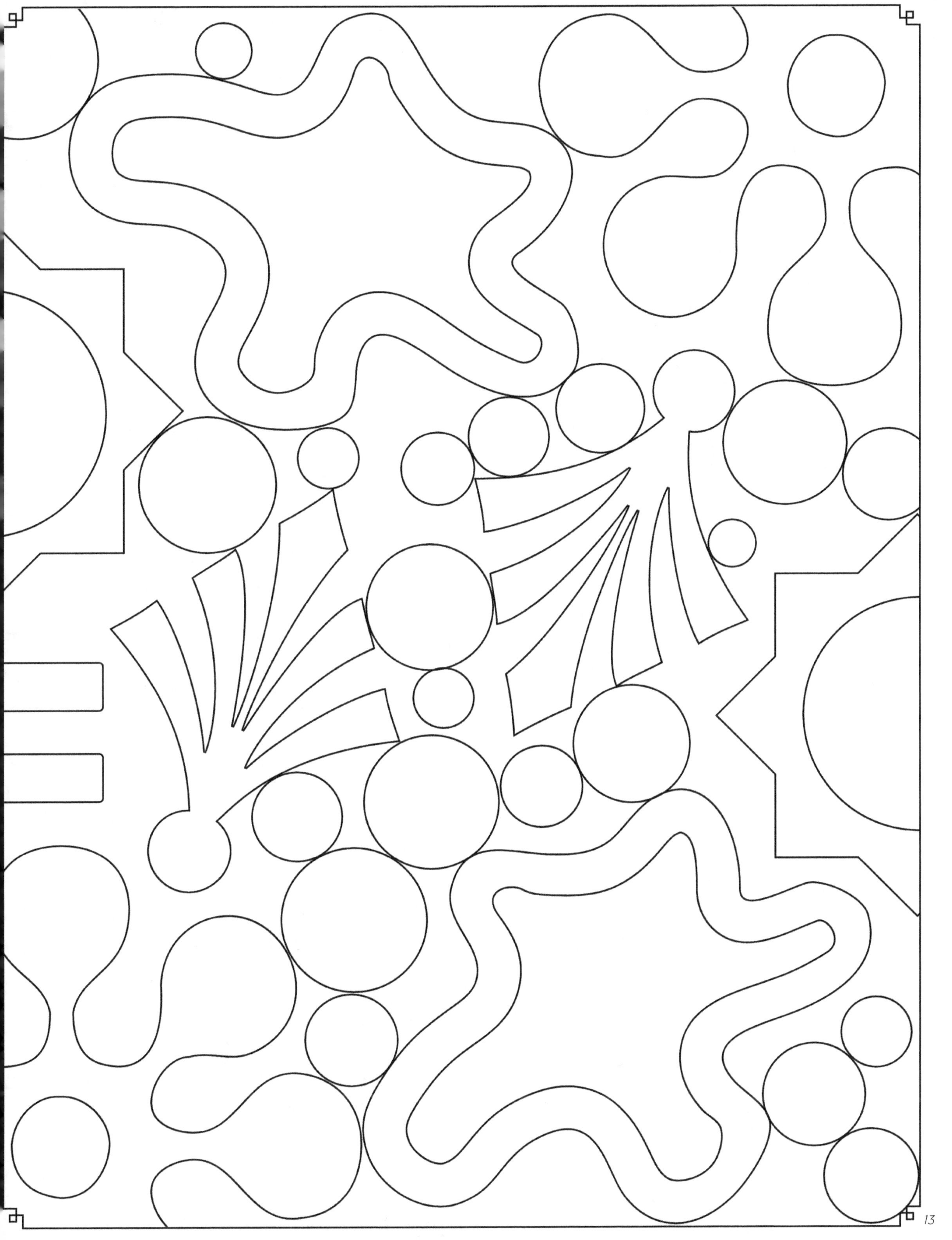

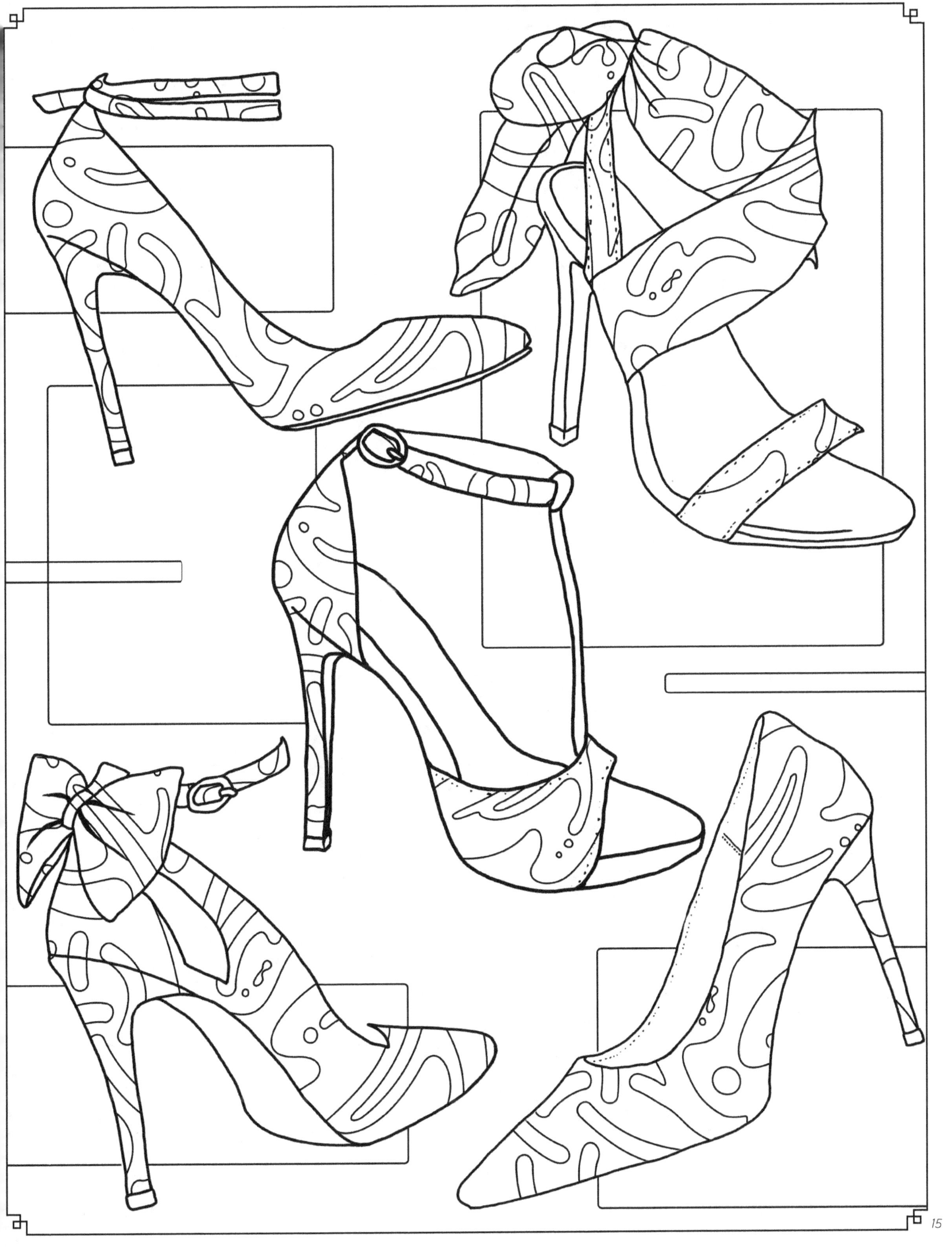

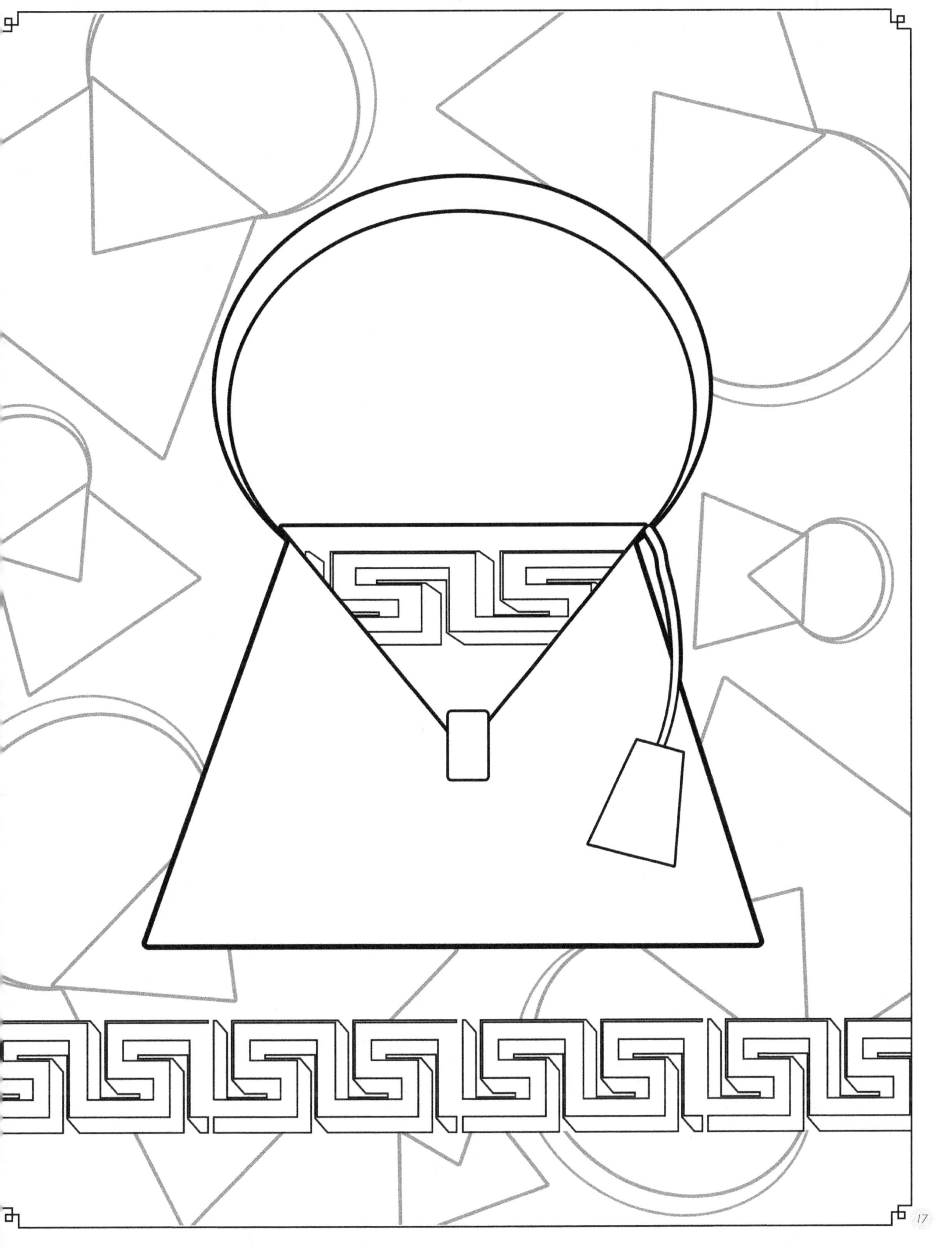

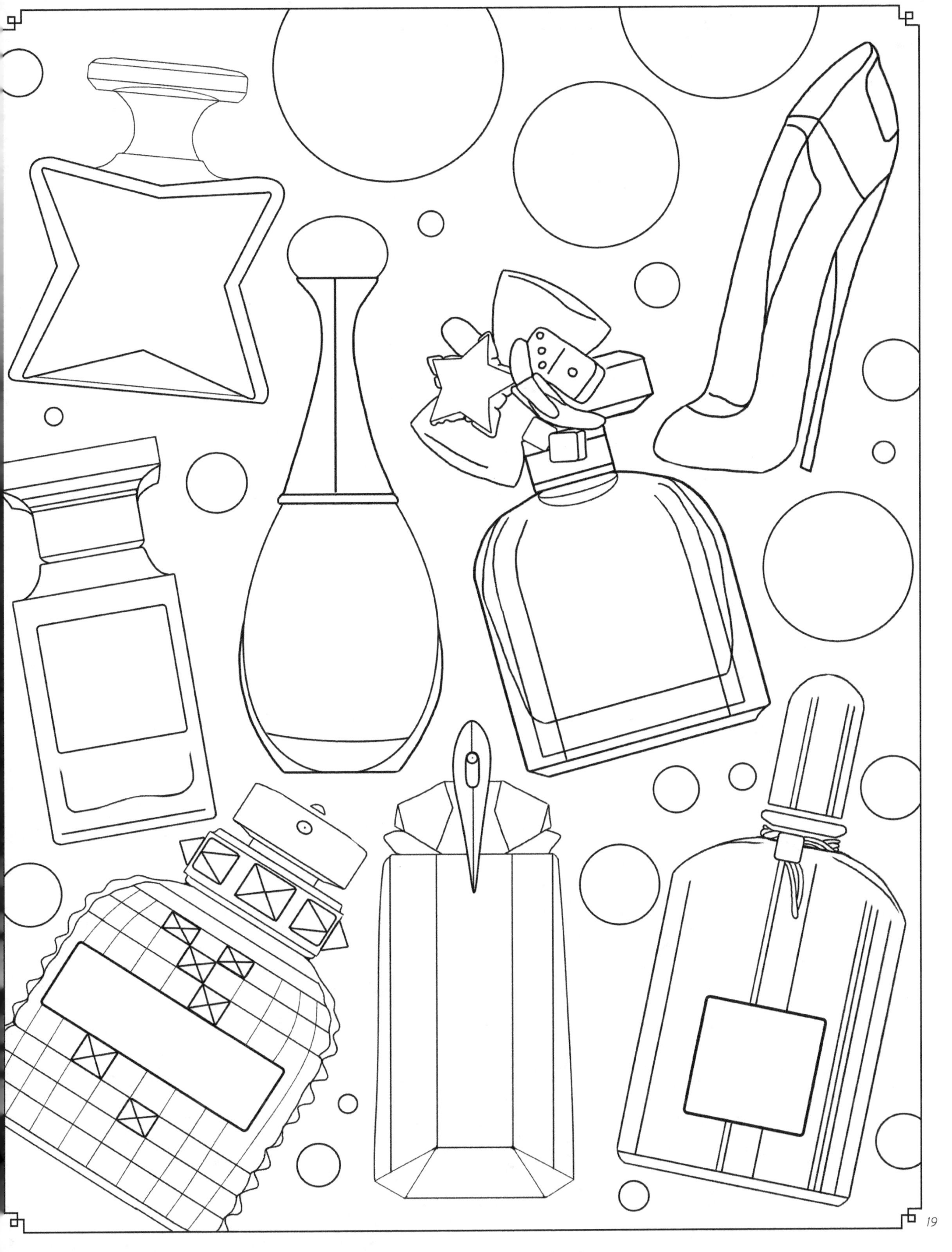

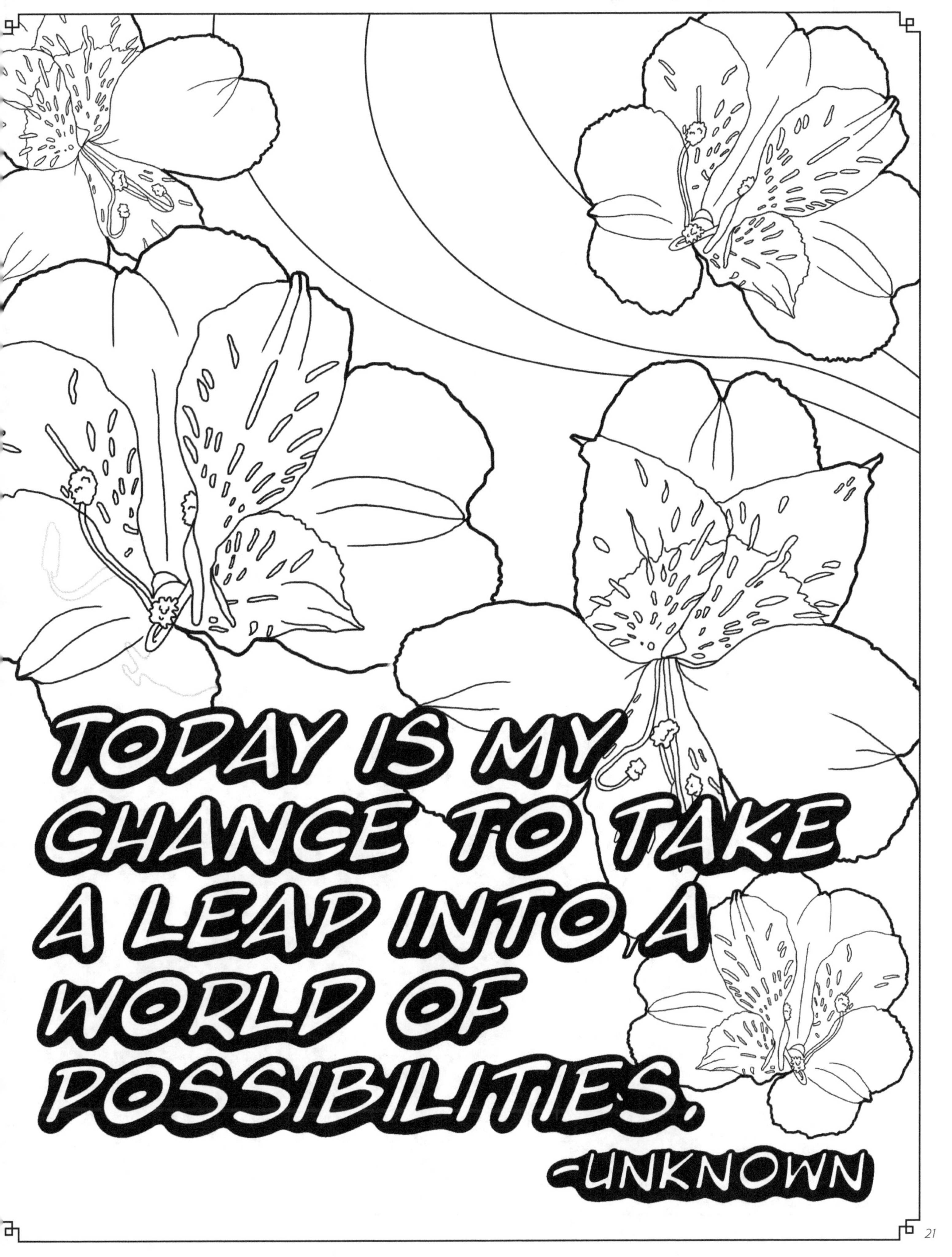

TODAY IS MY CHANCE TO TAKE A LEAP INTO A WORLD OF POSSIBILITIES.
-UNKNOWN

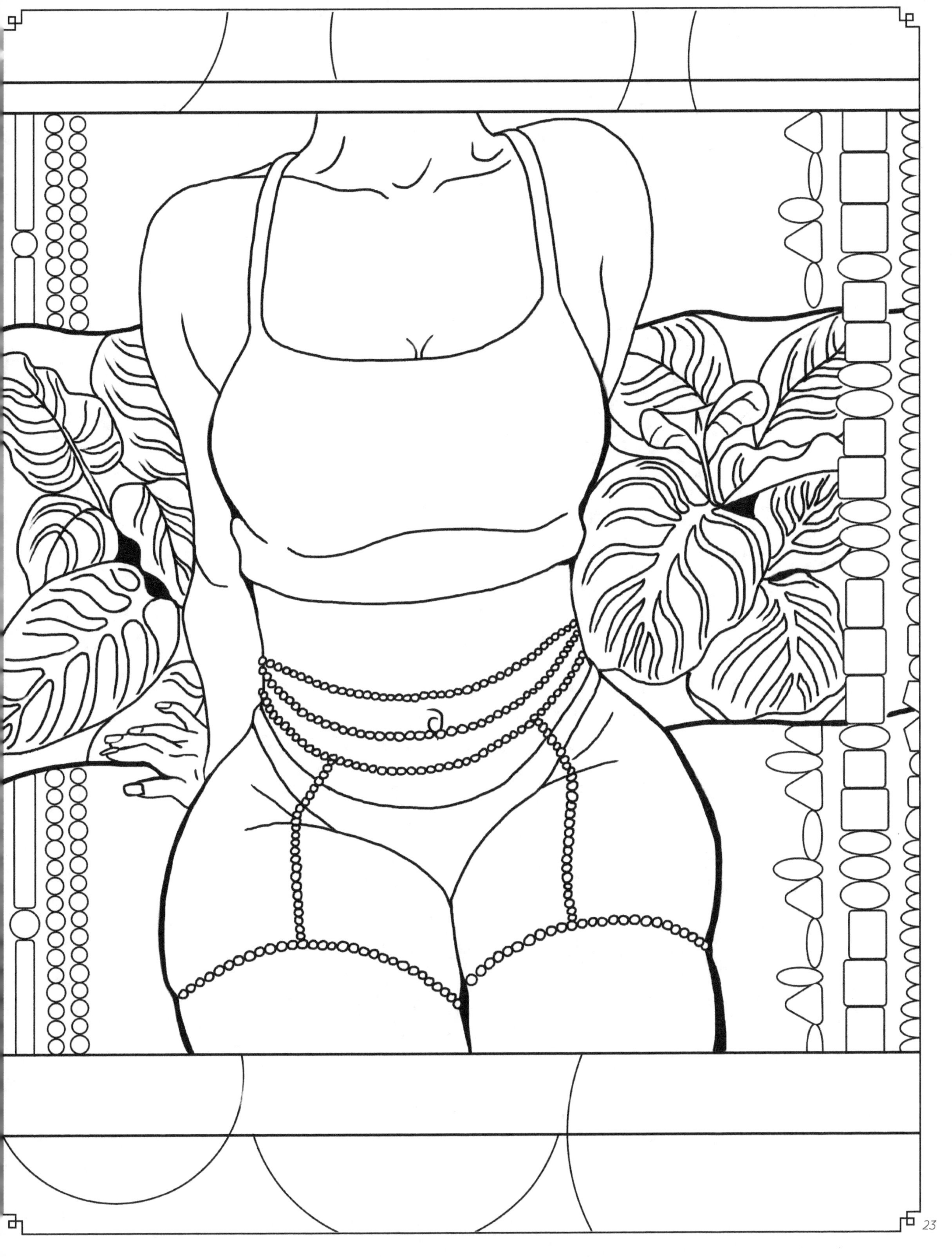

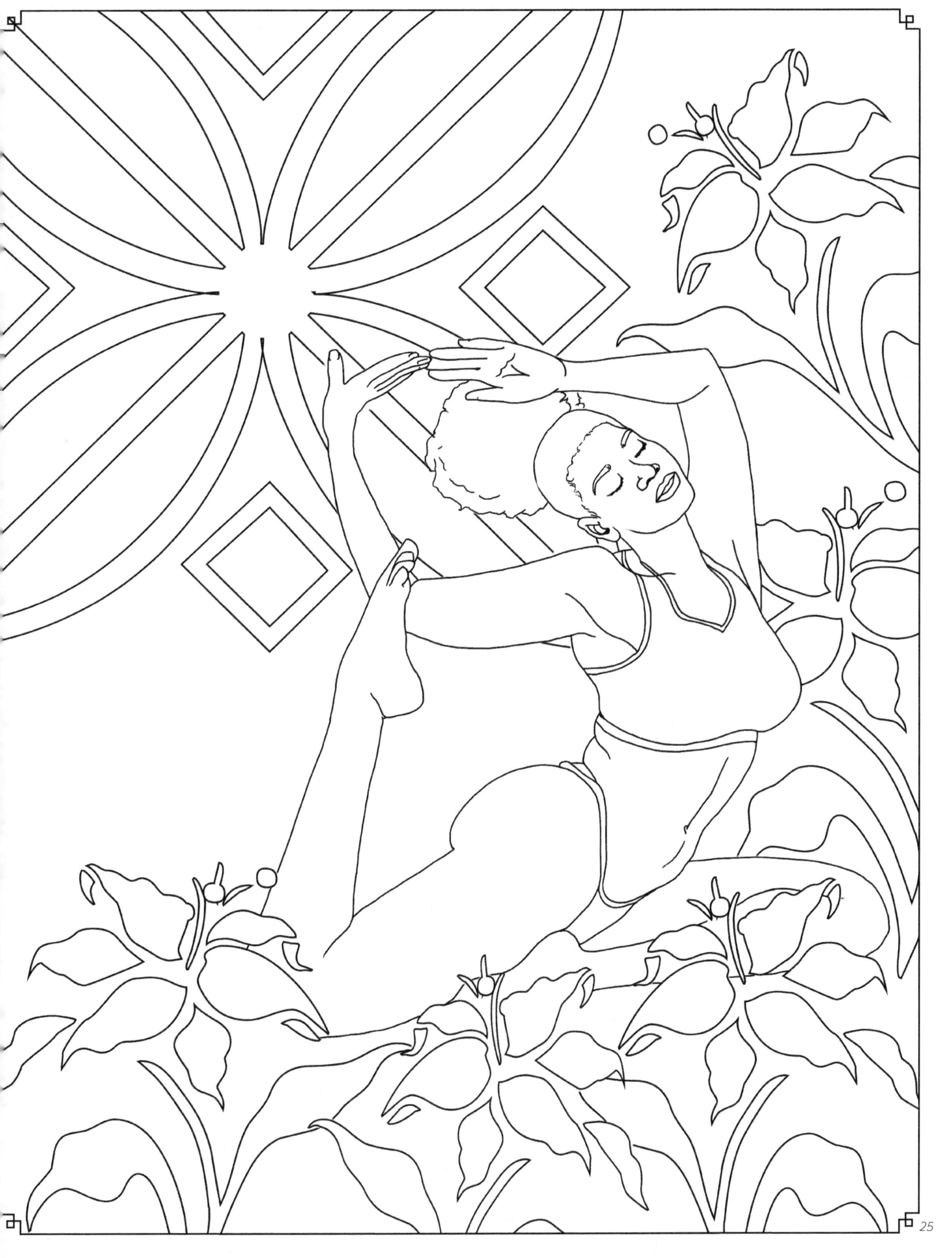

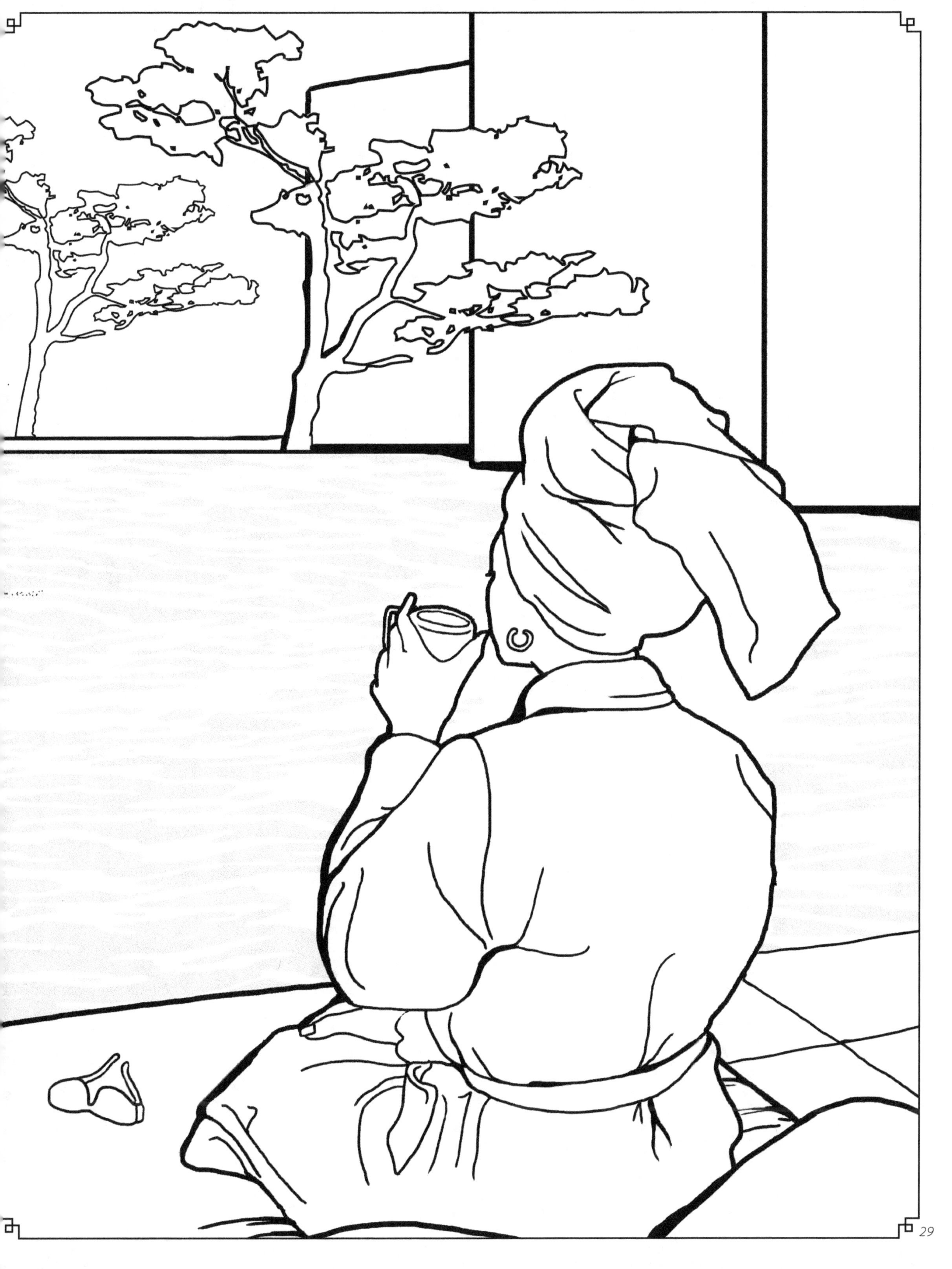

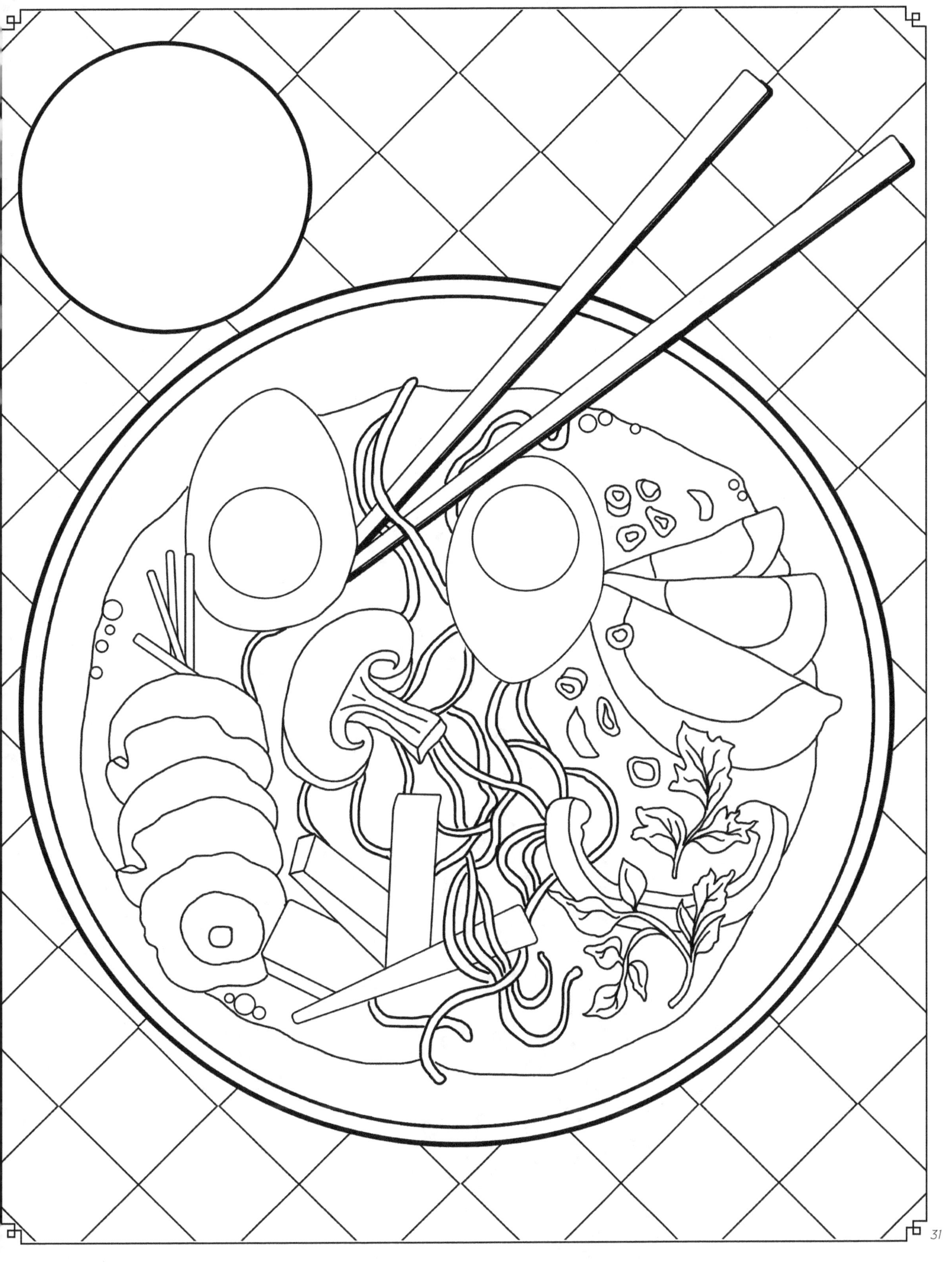

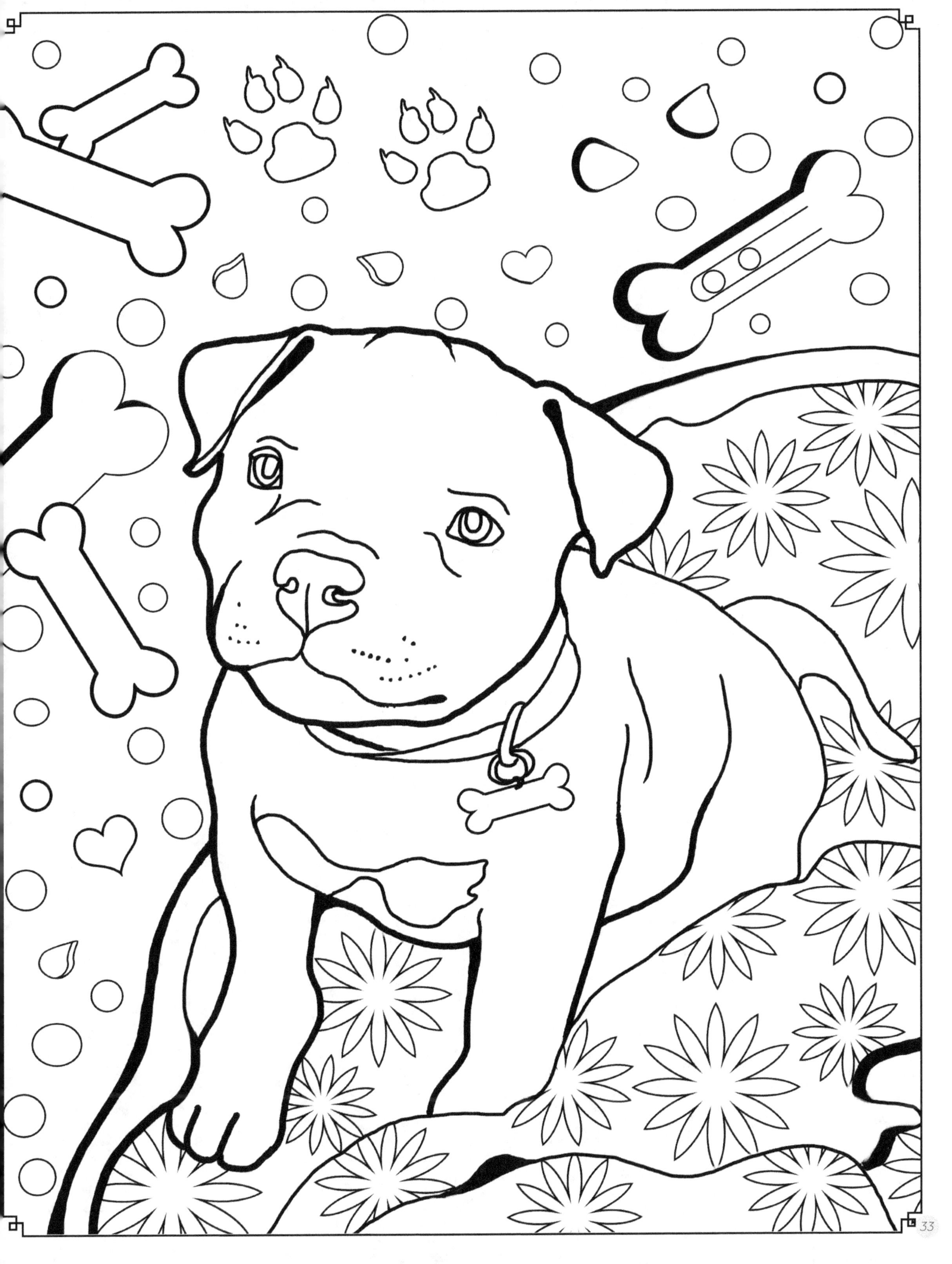

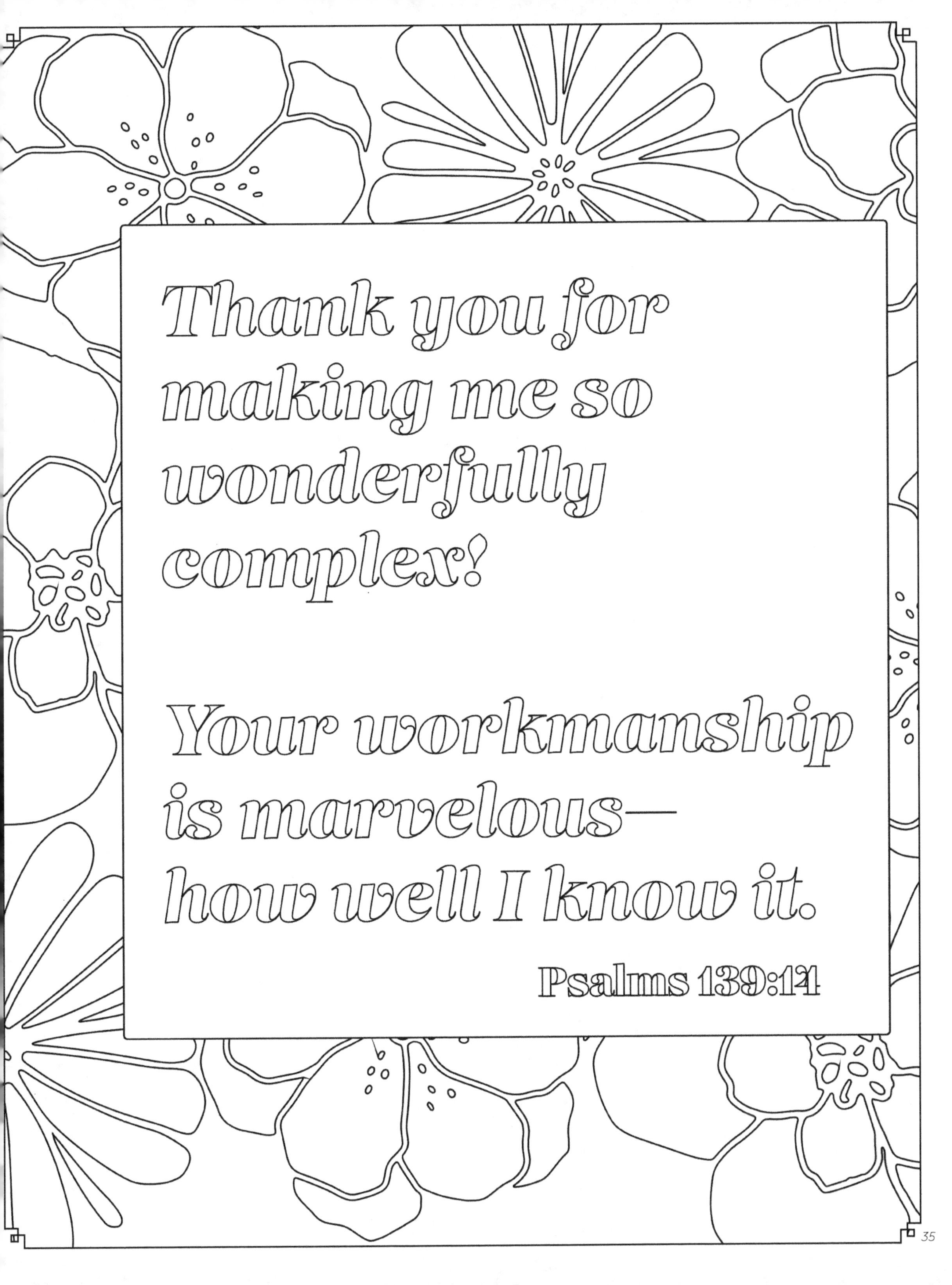

Thank you for making me so wonderfully complex!

Your workmanship is marvelous— how well I know it.

Psalms 139:14

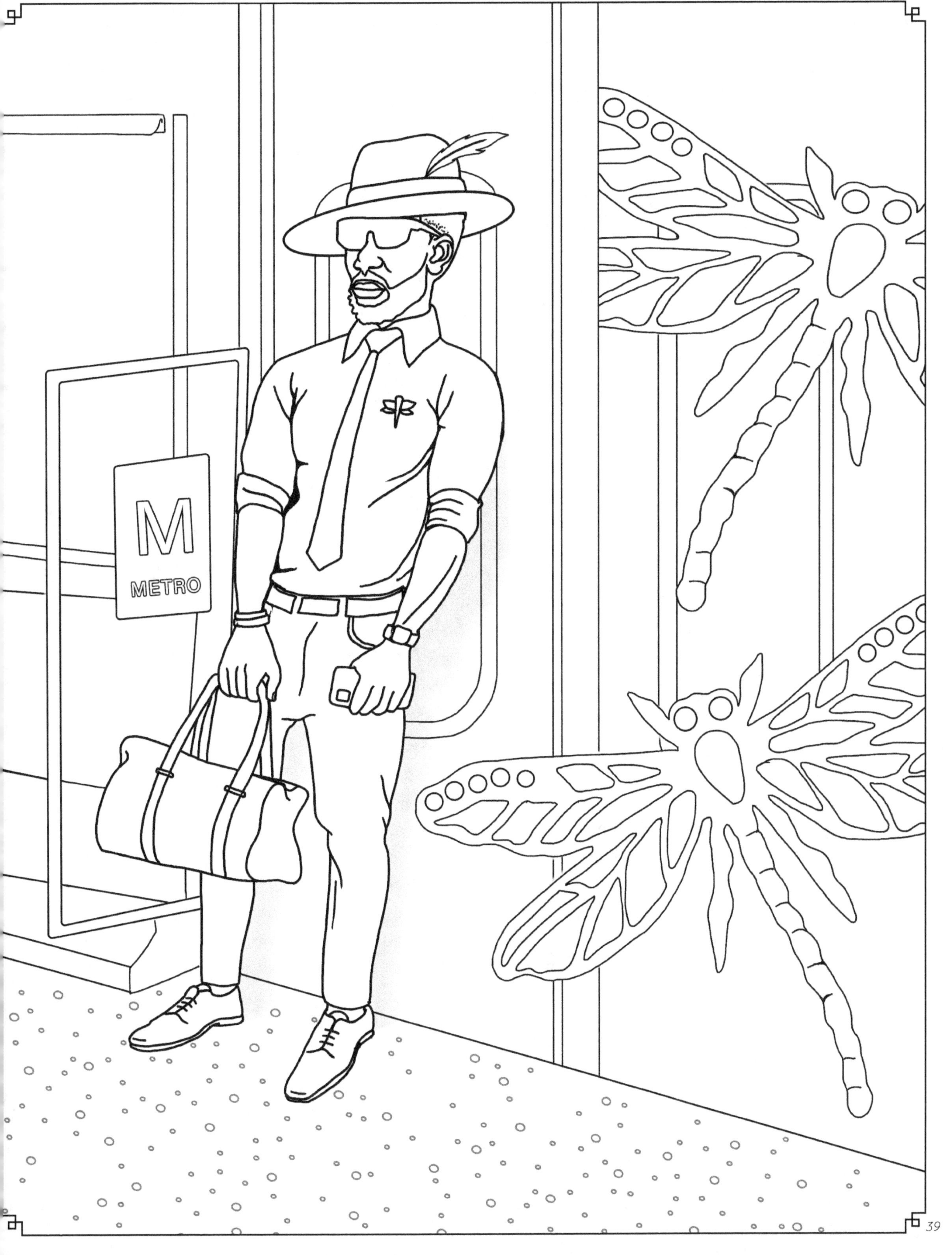

M
METRO

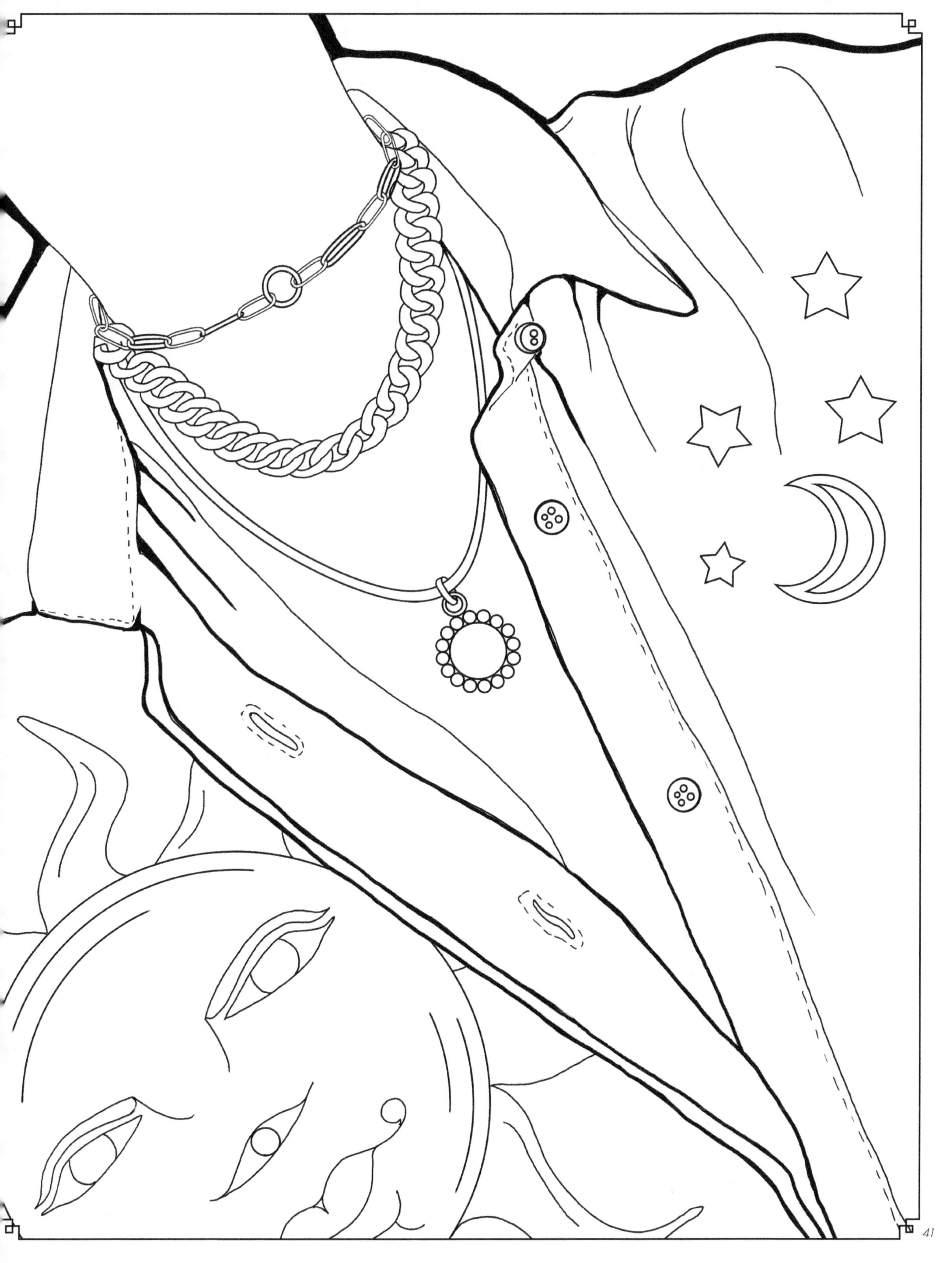

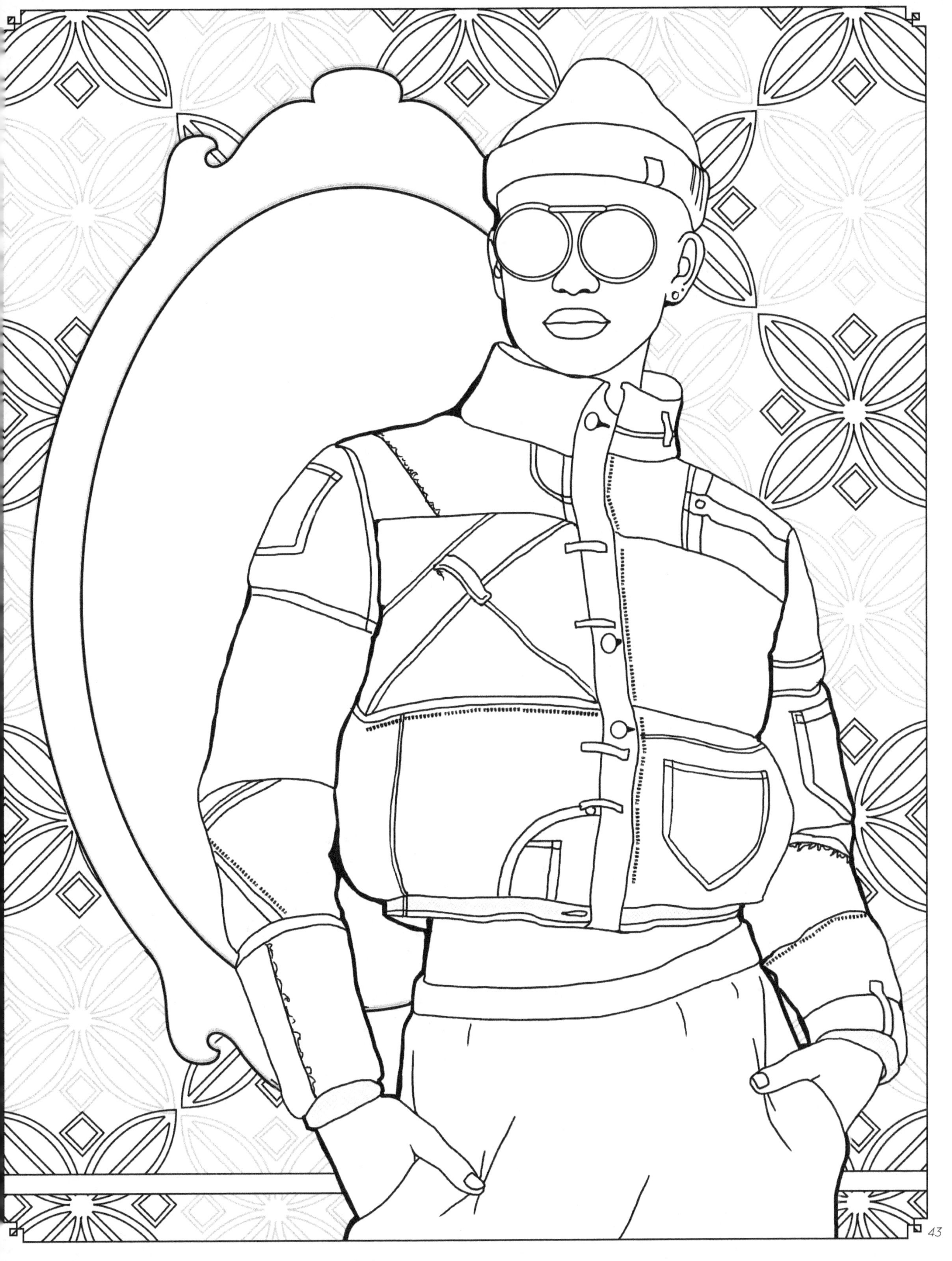

"SOMETIMES IT ENDS UP DIFFERENT AND IT IS BETTER THAT WAY."

-UNKNOWN

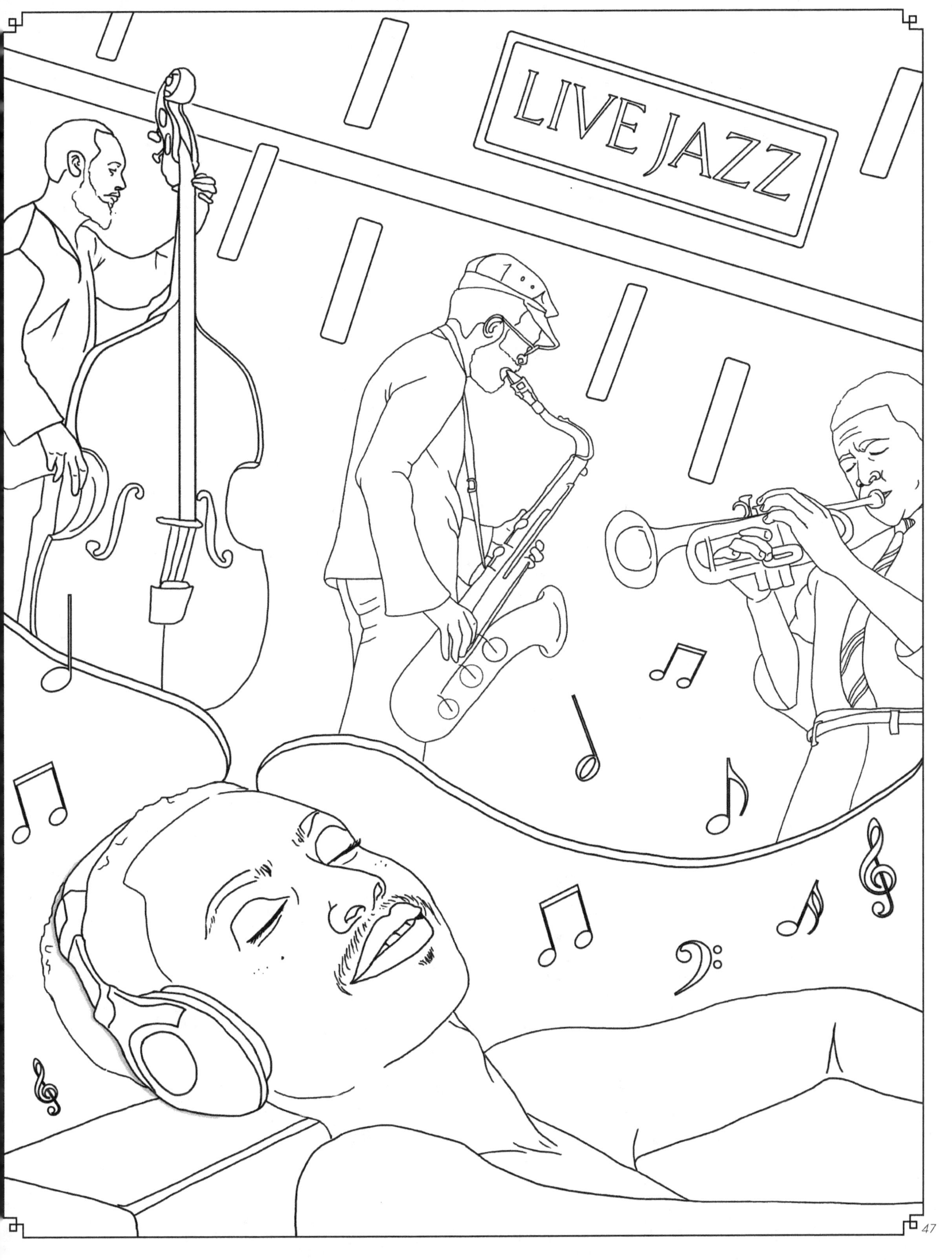

LIVE JAZZ

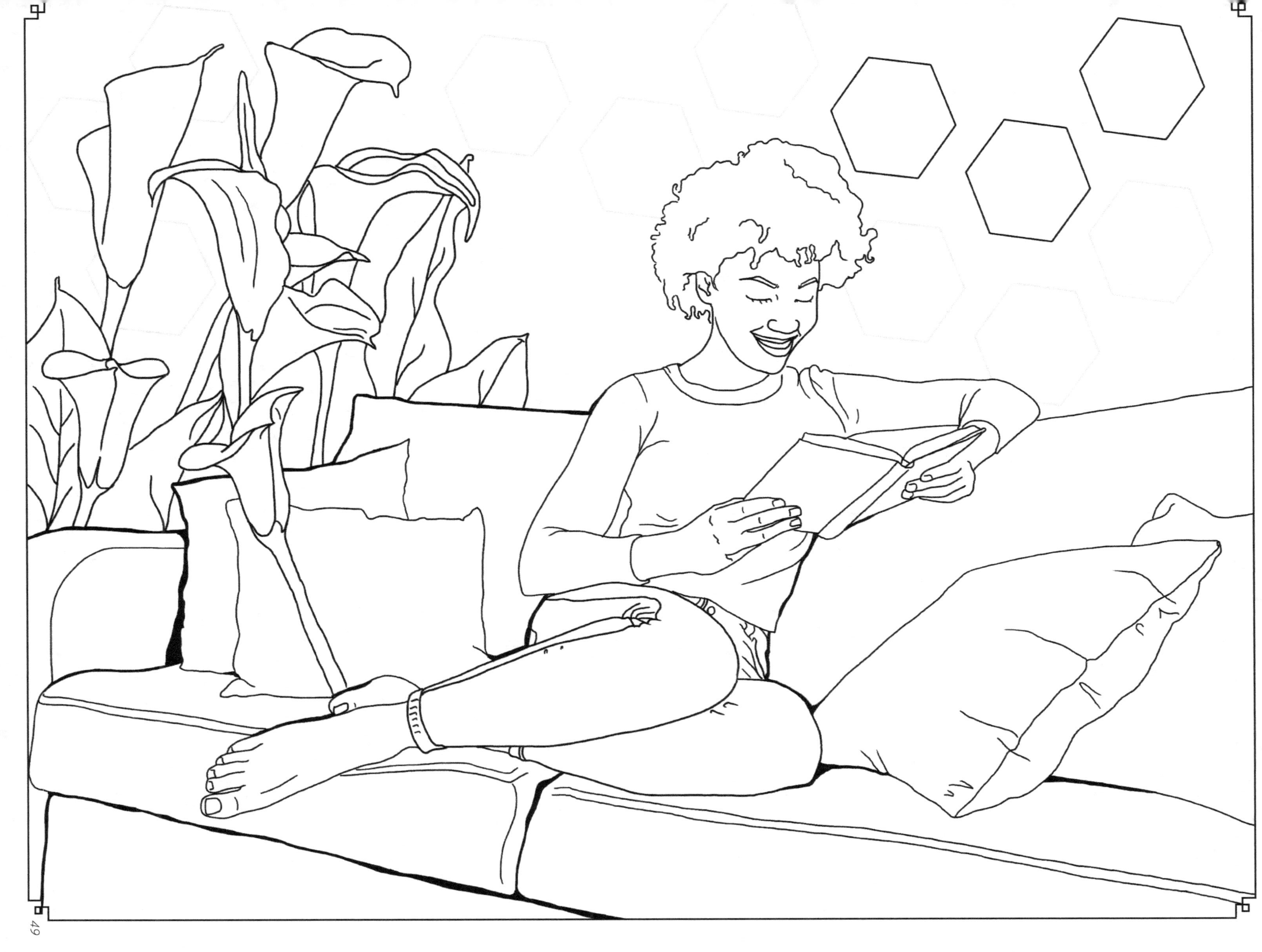

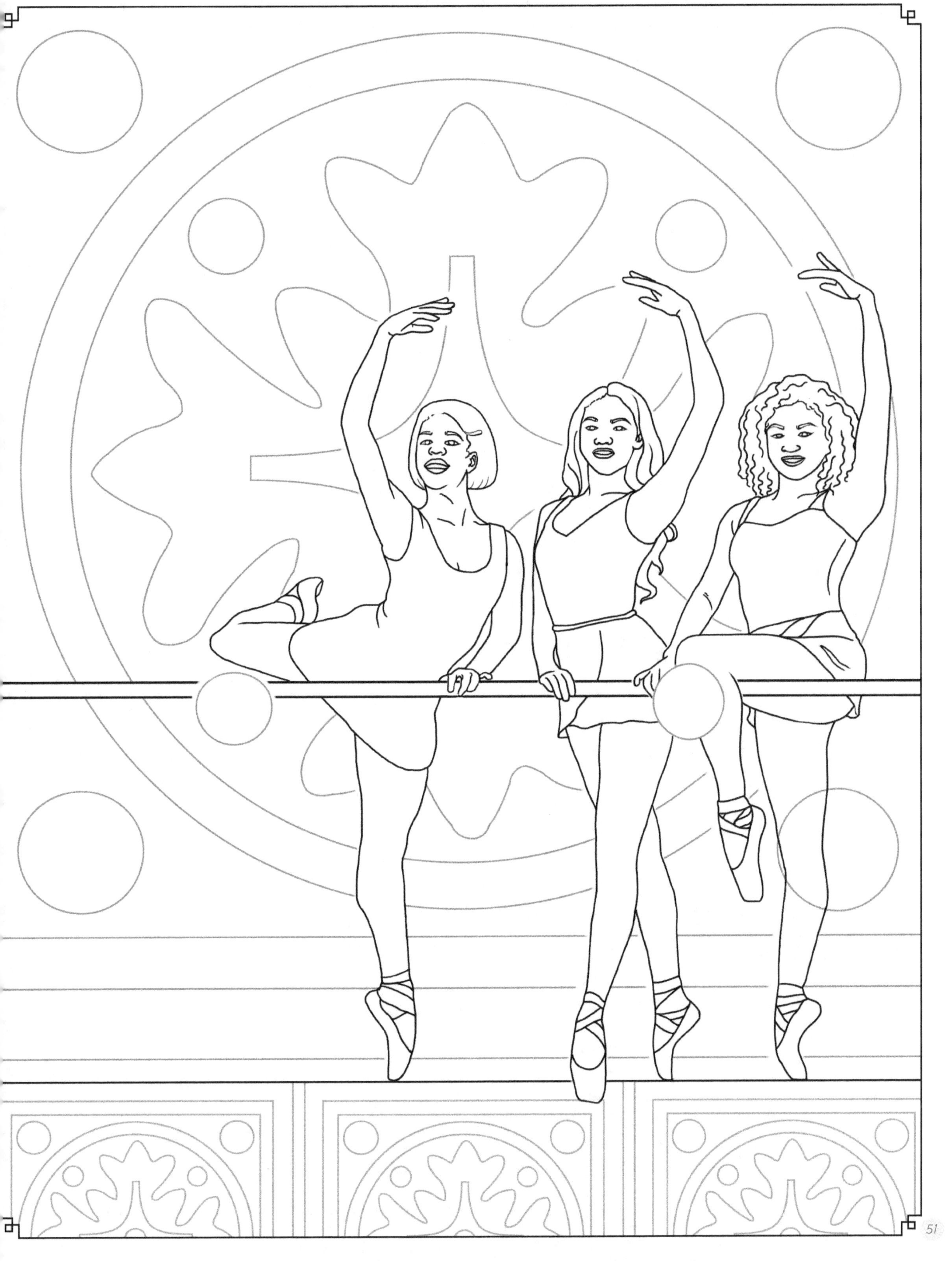

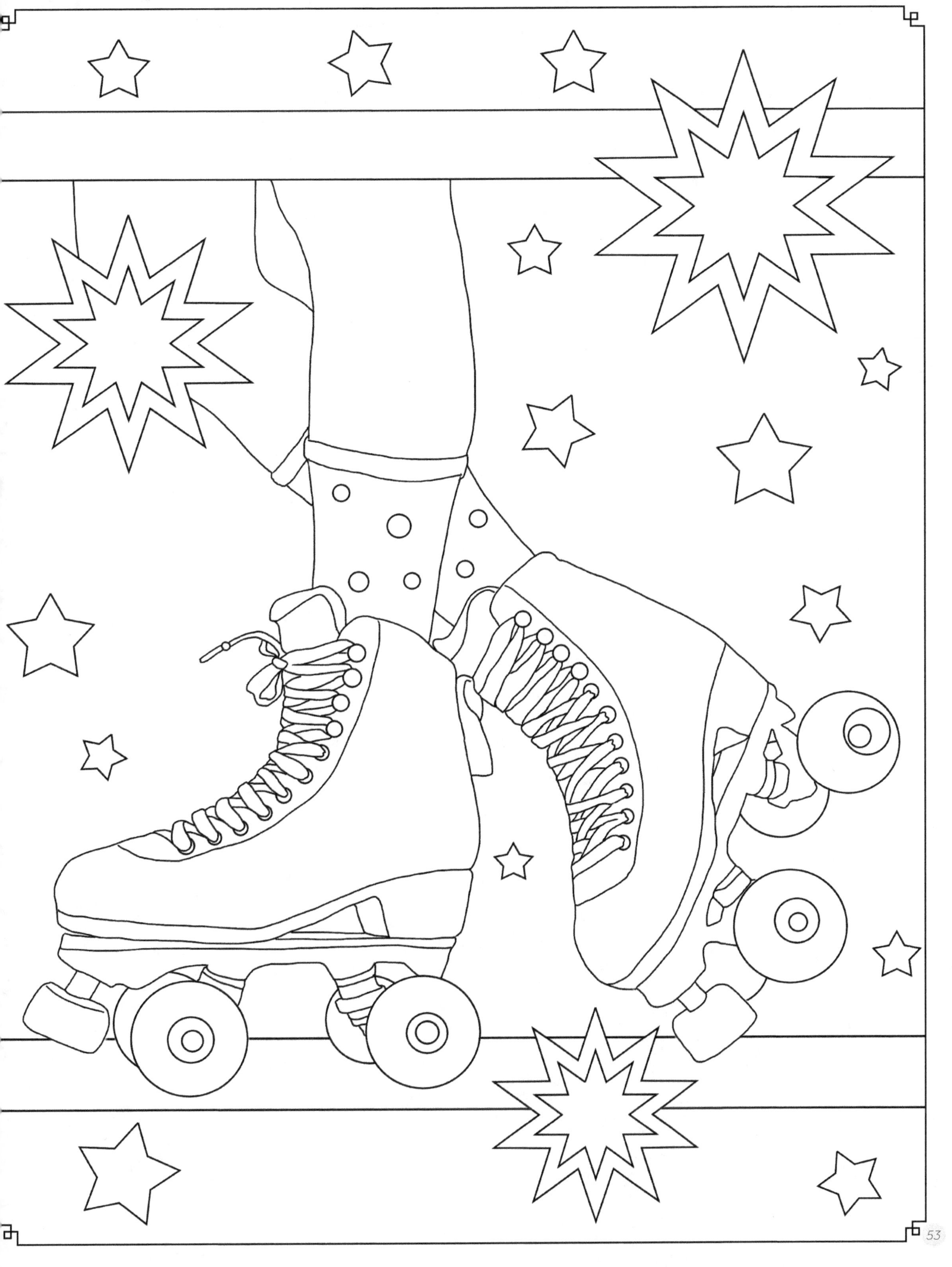

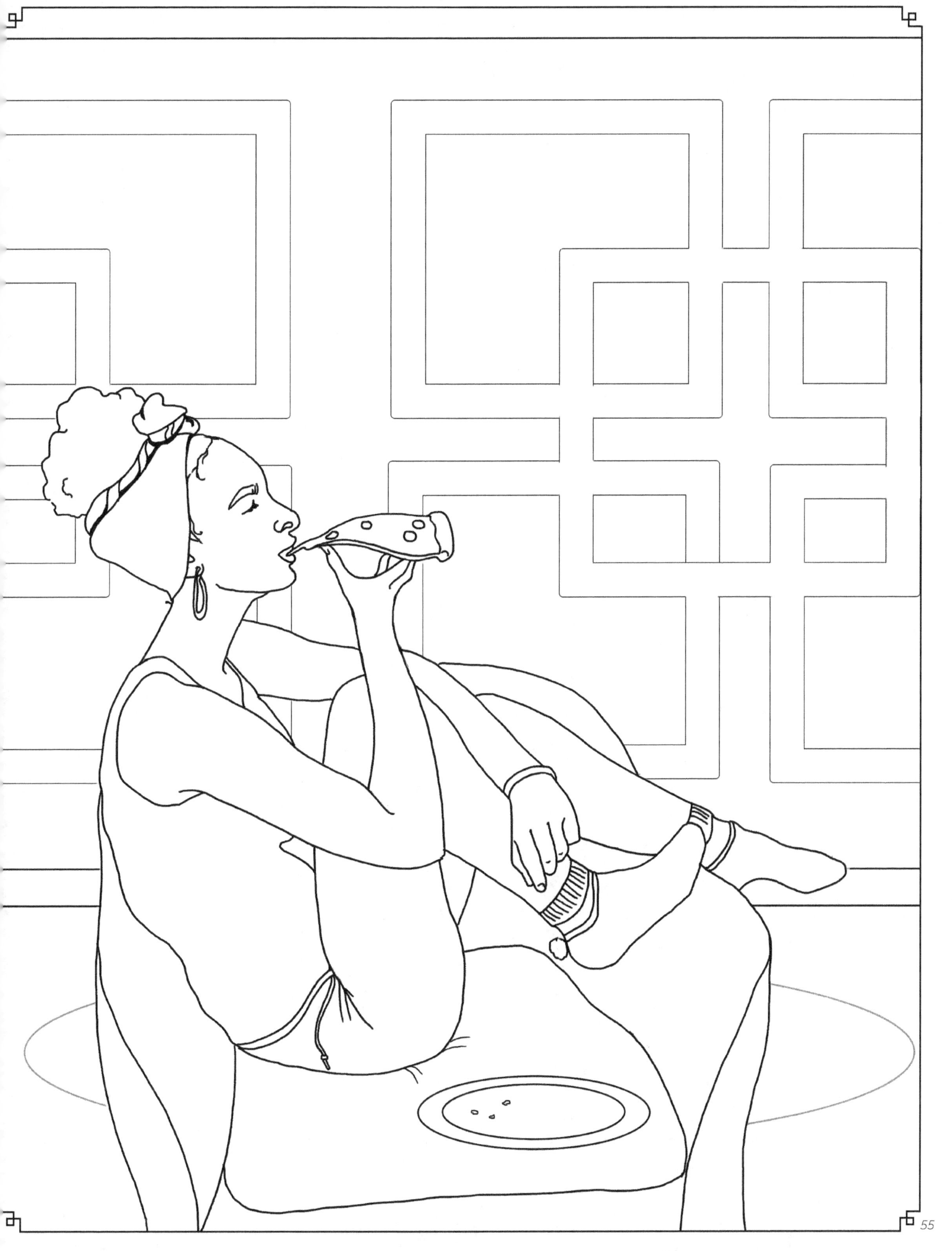

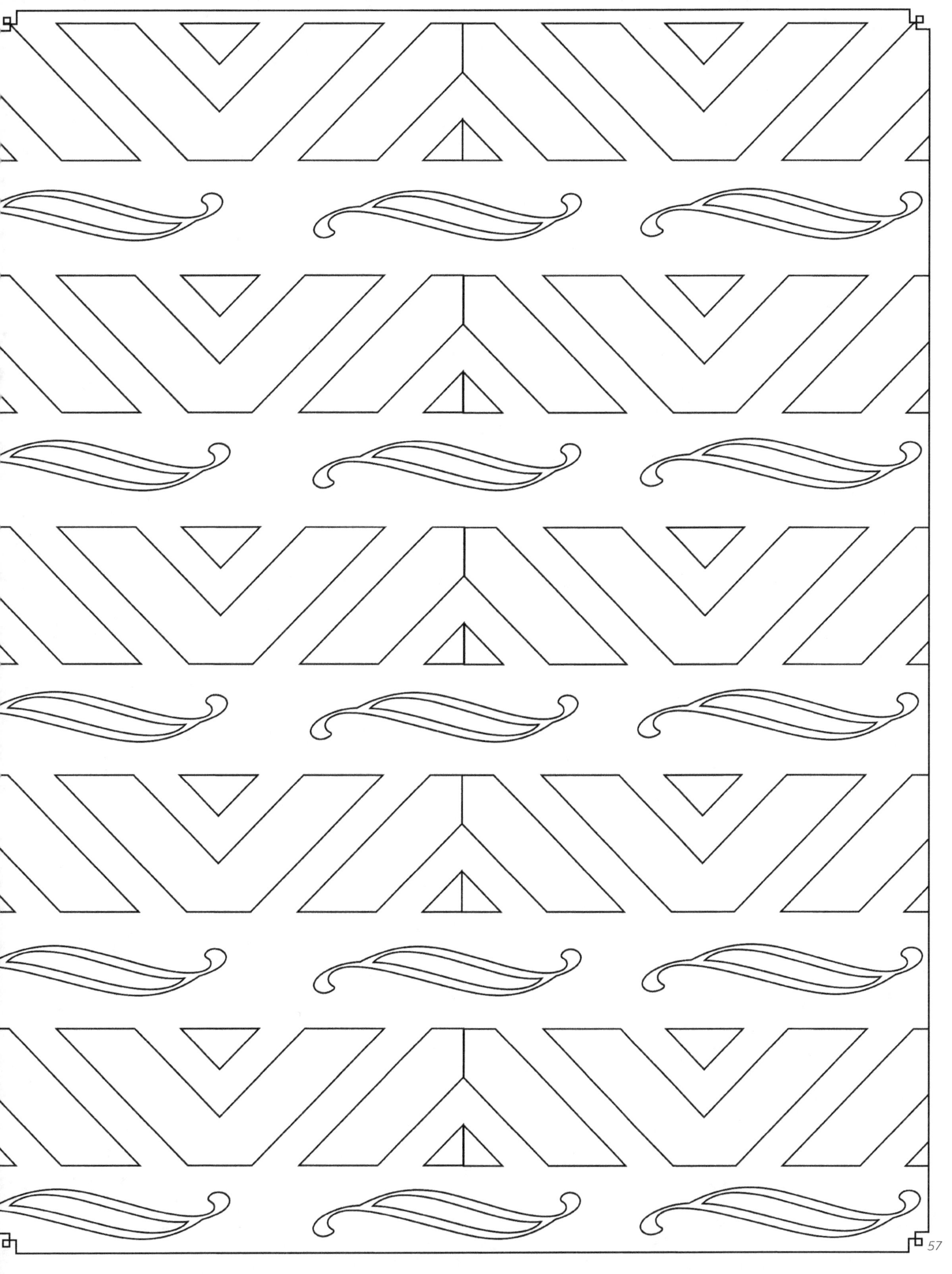

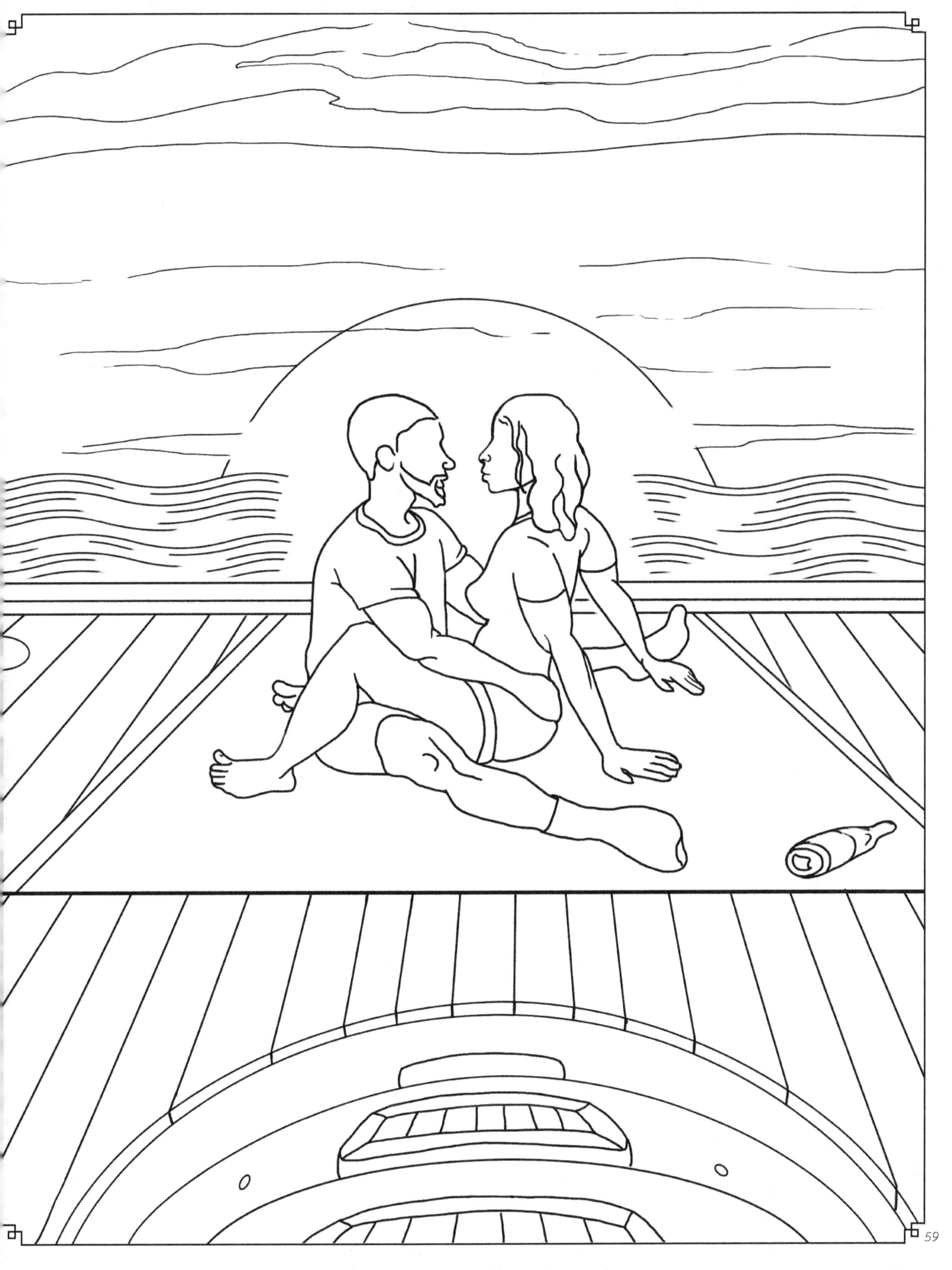

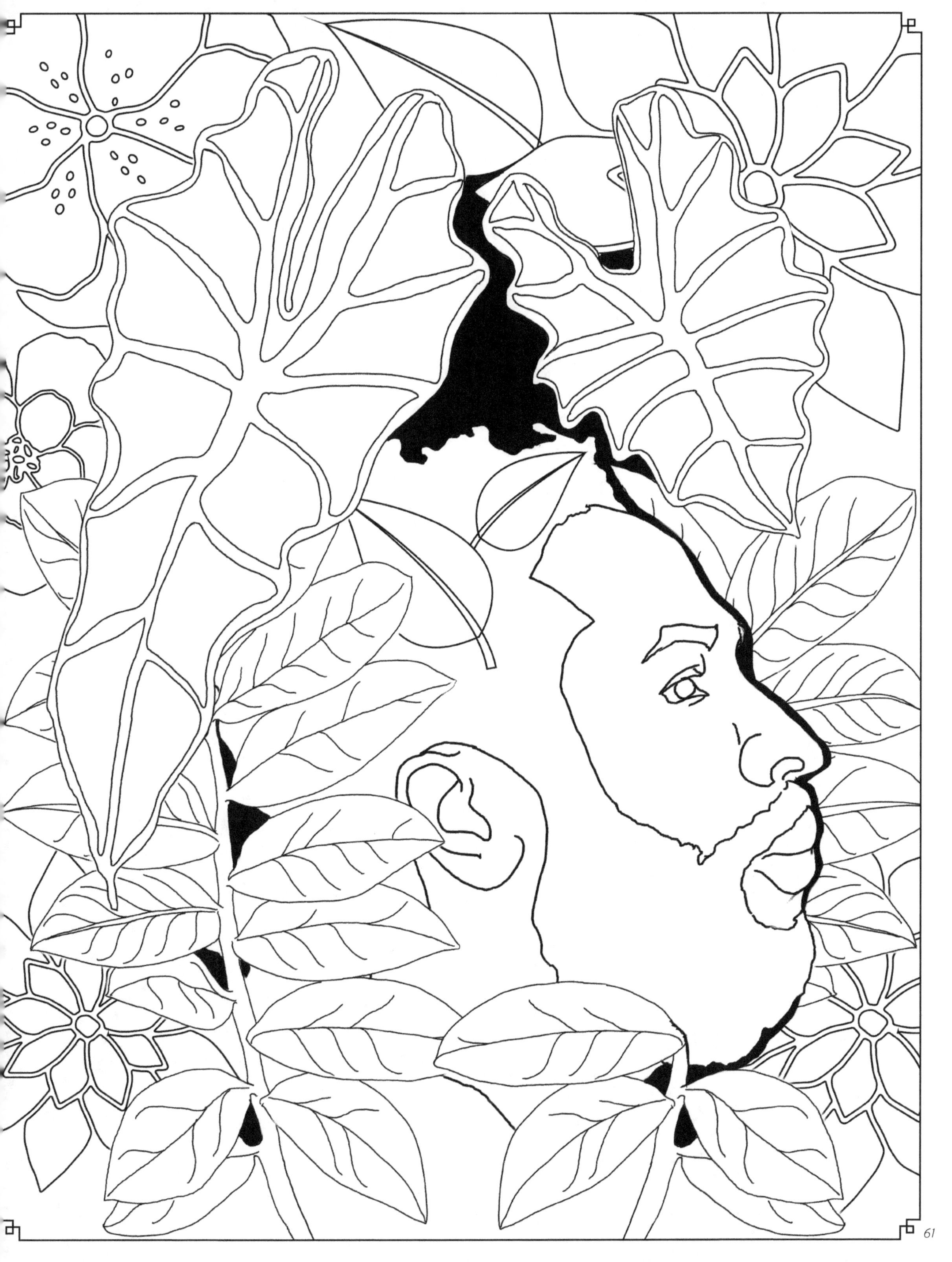

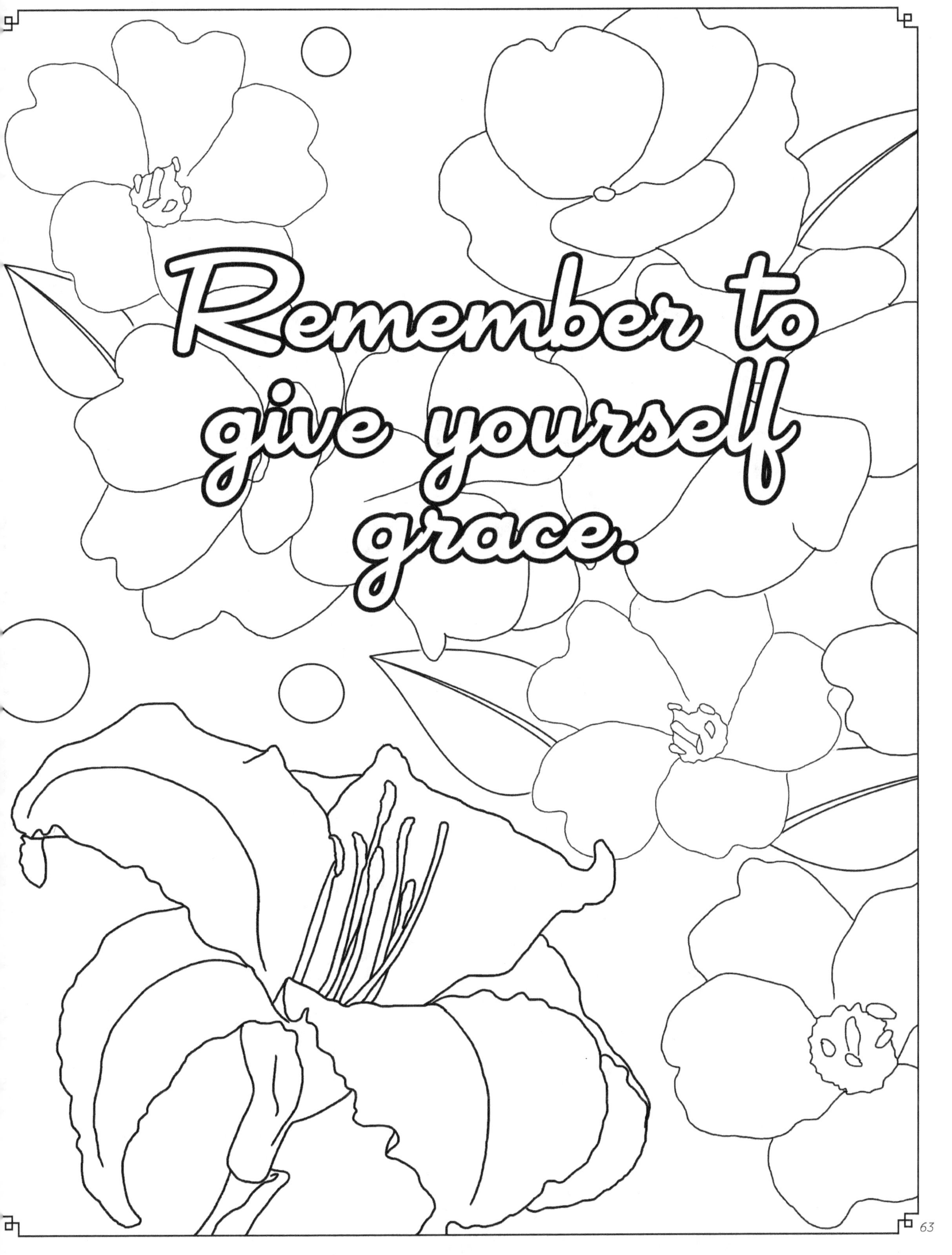

Remember to give yourself grace.

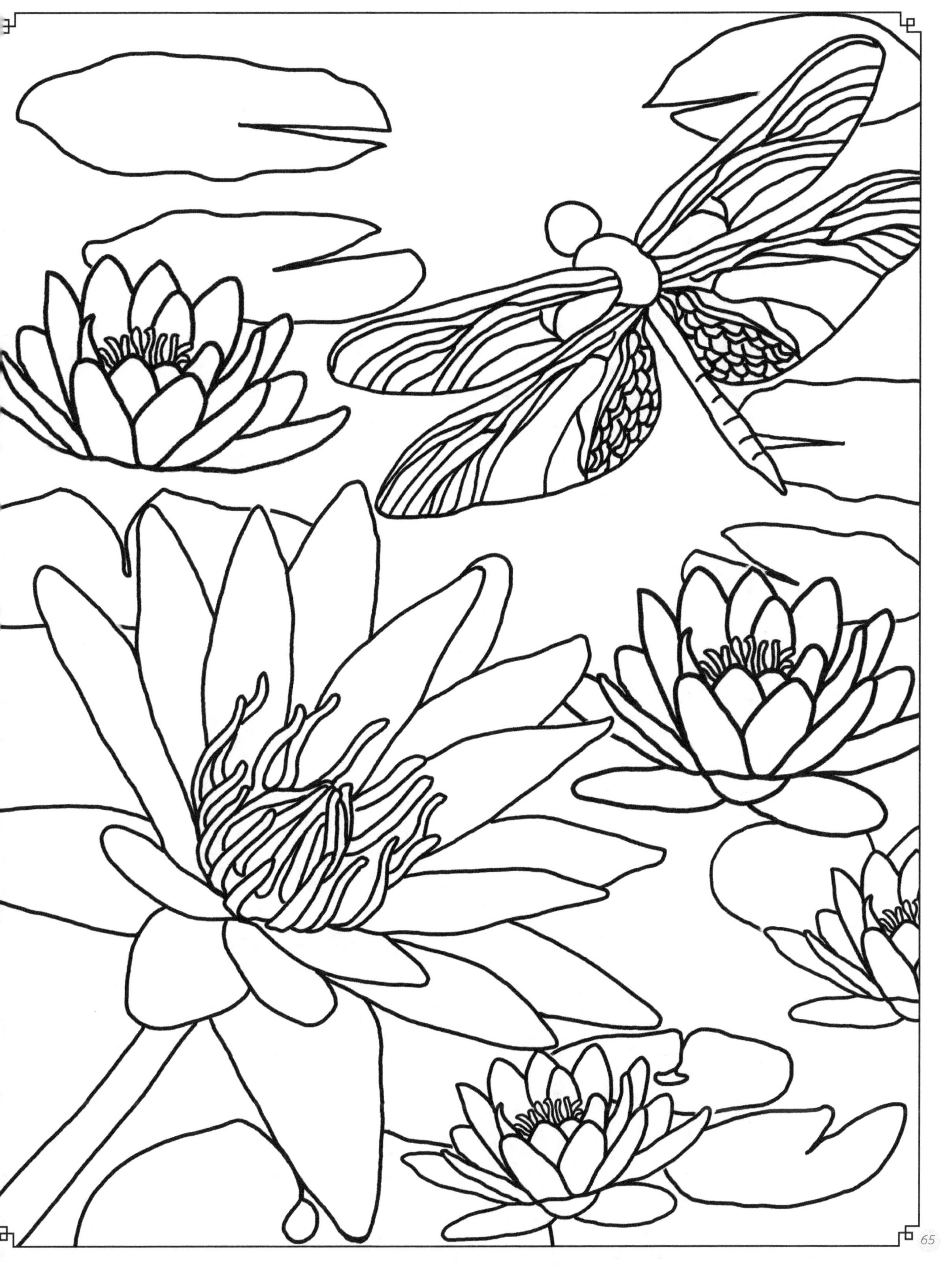

**Here is space for you to sketch, doodle, or draw what makes you happy and full.
You were born with the power to create.**

ABOUT THE ARTIST

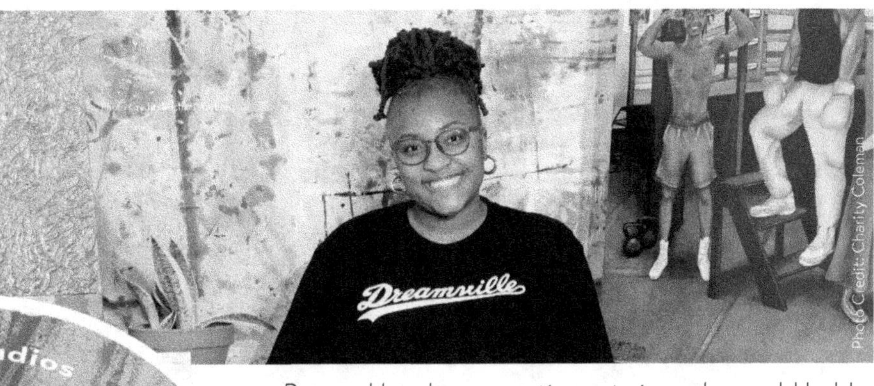

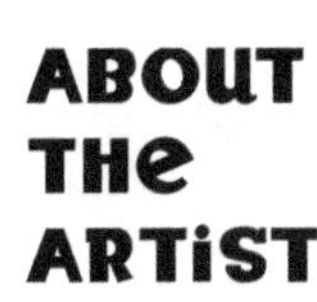

Racquel has been creating art since she could hold a crayon. It's something that continues to put a smile on her face. Racquel's artistic style is a brush of mono-chromatic, realistic portraiture that showcases black family, love, and excellence.

Her work has been showcased in several domestic and international exhibitions, a few community murals, and featured in prestigious venues; including the Congo Embassy in Paris. Racquel holds a MPS in the Business of Art and Design from Maryland Institute College of Art, a BA in Visual Arts & Design, and a BS in Visual Media & Design from North Carolina Agricultural and Technical State University.

www.ingramcontent.com/pod-product-compliance
Lightning Source LLC
Chambersburg PA
CBHW081229130726
47997CB00009B/2821